GERMS AND DISEASE

WHAT IS GERM WARFARE?

By Kathryn Kroe

Cavendish Square
New York

Published in 2023 by Cavendish Square Publishing, LLC
29 East 21st Street, New York, NY 10010

Website: cavendishsq.com

Disclaimer: Portions of this work were originally authored by Margaux Baum and Amy Romano and published as *Germ Warfare*. All new material this edition authored by Kathryn Kroe.

Library of Congress Cataloging-in-Publication Data

Names: Kroe, Kathryn, author.
Title: What is germ warfare? / Kathryn Kroe.
Description: New York : Cavendish Square Publishing, [2023] | Series: Germs and disease | Includes index.
Identifiers: LCCN 2021055539 | ISBN 9781502665317 (library binding) | ISBN 9781502665300 (paperback) | ISBN 9781502665324 (ebook)
Subjects: LCSH: Biological warfare--Juvenile literature. | Biological weapons--Juvenile literature.
Classification: LCC UG447.8 .K76 2023 | DDC 358/.38--dc23/eng/20211123
LC record available at https://lccn.loc.gov/2021055539

Editor: Kathryn Kroe
Copyeditor: Jane Katirgis
Designer: Andrea Davison-Bartolotta

The photographs in this book are used by permission and through the courtesy of: Cover ChameleonsEye/Shutterstock.com; series art backgrounds CHIARI VFX/Shutterstock.com; pp. 4–5 Gorodenkoff/Shutterstock.com; p. 6 Hoika Mikhail/Shutterstock.com; p. 7 Garmasheva Natalia/Shutterstock.com; p. 8 courtesy of the Library of Congress; p. 10 James Jiao/Shutterstock.com; p. 11 Damian Pankowiec/Shutterstock.com; p. 12 Peddalanka Ramesh Babu/Shutterstock.com; p. 15 Rick Bowmer/AP Images; p. 16 maimoon/Shutterstock.com; p. 18 Everett Collection/Shutterstock.com; p. 21 Gavin Baker Photography/Shutterstock.com; p. 22 TommyB_Photo/Shutterstock.com; p. 23 Moravian/Shutterstock.com; p. 26 (background) NicoElNino/Shutterstock.com; p. 26 (symbol) konstantinks/Shutterstock.com; p. 28 Rob Hainer/Shutterstock.com; p. 30 alexfan32/Shutterstock.com; p. 31 Michelle Lee Photography/Shutterstock.com; p. 32 Pixsooz/Shutterstock.com; p. 34 MAMIAE T8/Shutterstock.com; p. 37 Vitaliy Holovin/Shutterstock.com; p. 39 Rob Crandall/Shutterstock.com.

CPSIA compliance information: Batch #CSCSQ23: For further information contact Cavendish Square Publishing LLC, New York, New York, at 1-877-980-4450.

Printed in the United States of America

CONTENTS

INTRODUCTION

When you hear the word "warfare," you may think of missile attacks or soldiers with physical weapons fighting on a battlefield. There is another type of weapon, however, that can also be horribly destructive. Biological weapons, used in what is commonly referred to as germ warfare (or biological warfare), can be **weapons of mass destruction** (WMDs). Most germs don't often scare us. We know how to protect ourselves and have our immune systems as a backup. When germs are used as weapons, though, they can catch us defenseless.

Although germ warfare has existed throughout history, it has rarely been used in the 20th and 21st centuries. However, the idea of it still inspires fear, likely because people dislike being sick or have seen someone they know suffer from serious illness.

The risk of biological warfare remains small, but it is still a real danger. Bioweapons exist and have been produced and sometimes **stockpiled** by governments all around the world. It is helpful for governments and citizens to understand the risk of these weapons and be able to identify strategies to stay safe.

Dangerous germs can be studied with microscopes, increasing our knowledge but also increasing the risk they could be used as weapons.

Poisoned arrows are some of the earliest examples of germ warfare. Even if the arrow itself did not kill the enemy, the idea was that the poison, or germs, would.

CHAPTER 1

WHEN DID GERM WARFARE BEGIN?

Ever since humans have been fighting, they have used poisons against their enemies. Once scientists Louis Pasteur and Robert Koch made the connection between microbes and disease, biological weapons could be chosen and designed more specifically. Biological warfare, or a biological attack, refers to intentionally releasing a **pathogen** or **biotoxin** in order to harm humans, plants, or animals.

Dating back to 400 BCE, Greek armies used arrows dipped into the flesh or blood of decomposing bodies to create poisoned weapons. Roman and Persian soldiers poisoned water supplies by dumping dead animals into enemy wells. In the 1340s CE, forces known as Tatars attacked the city of Caffa (sometimes spelled Kaffa) in today's Ukraine and hurled bodies infected with bubonic plague over the city walls, hoping to spread the disease to the local population.

Parts of this ancient fortress of Caffa still stand today, but they weren't enough to keep germ warfare out.

SMALLPOX AND WAR

During the French and Indian War (1754–1763), Native American warriors laid siege to an outpost called Fort Pitt. Besides being under siege, British soldiers were worried smallpox would spread from the outpost hospital through the cramped population. The Fort Pitt commander wrote to his superior, Sir Jeffrey Amherst, who was the commander in chief of the British forces in North America. In a written account of his reply, Amherst suggested, "Could it not be contrived to Send the Small Pox among those Disaffected Tribes of Indians? We must, on this occasion, Use Every Stratagem in our power to Reduce them." Amherst and the British troops intended to use biological warfare to wipe out Native warriors.

This is among a list of tactics throughout history used against the Native Americans. Research, however, suggests that plans to use blankets and handkerchiefs "infected" with smallpox may not have been an effective means of spreading the germs. Furthermore, the smallpox spreading in Fort Pitt could have come from the Native Americans in the first place, as smallpox was circulating in their population at the time. Regardless of its success or failure, the brutality of the intentions will not be forgotten.

Sir Jeffrey Amherst may have been behind an idea to use germ warfare to wipe out Native American adversaries of the British.

EARLY GERM WARFARE

1155 CE: Emperor Barbarossa poisons water wells with human bodies in Tortona, Italy.

1346: Tatars catapult bodies of plague victims over the city walls of Caffa on the Crimean Peninsula.

1495: The Spanish mix wine with the blood of leprosy patients to sell to their French foes.

1650: The Polish fire saliva from rabid dogs toward their enemies.

1675: The first deal is struck between German and French forces not to use "poison bullets."

1763: The British distribute blankets from smallpox patients to Native Americans in the French and Indian War.

1797: Napoleon floods the plains around Mantua, Italy, to enhance the spread of malaria.

1863: Confederates sell clothing from yellow fever and smallpox patients to Union troops during the American Civil War.

Even before we had a strong understanding of germs, this timeline shows germ warfare was a commonly used tactic.

Beginnings of Sophisticated Germ Warfare

By the time of World War I (1914–1918), scientists had soundly established the germ theory of disease, documenting how bacteria and viruses transmit illness. During the last German offensive in 1918, scientists applied this theory in a widespread campaign of biological sabotage, hoping to avoid impending defeat by targeting livestock. They hoped to sicken cattle and sheep in Romania, the United

States, Argentina, Spain, and Norway, thus contaminating these countries' food supplies. Their efforts were largely unsuccessful. Germ warfare initiatives would really ramp up by the start of World War II (1939–1945).

Before and during World War II, the Japanese military practiced a much more refined and effective germ warfare. An infamous division of Japan's Imperial Army called Unit 731 began systematic biological attacks against China around 1936. Japanese scientists used humans—mostly peasants and prisoners in occupied Manchuria—to test a variety of lethal pathogens, including the bacteria that cause anthrax and the plague. It is estimated that as many as 10,000 people were killed.

By 1940, Japan's germ warfare efforts expanded to include the intentional introduction of plague-infested fleas, as well as the active contamination of wells and poisoning of food supplies, in several Chinese cities. Hundreds of thousands of people fell victim before Unit 731 dismantled and destroyed all evidence of the attacks.

Though biological warfare through water supplies is less likely to work today, in 1940s China, intentional contamination of wells such as this one caused many citizens to become ill.

THREATS DURING THE COLD WAR

The United States and the Soviet Union had a 45-year standoff known as the Cold War (1946–1991). During these years, the nations were technically at peace, but tensions remained high and both countries wanted to be seen as the most dominant nation in the world. Biological weapons programs reached a peak in both nations as a result. Both countries researched various ways to use bacteria, viruses, and biological toxins (poisons released by microorganisms) as weapons of war. This time, germ warfare programs not only tried to develop diseases, but also researched methods of dispersing deadly **agents**. Researchers in both countries developed biological agents as fine-mist **aerosols** and looked at ways to deliver them using bombs and missiles.

During the Cold War, scientists and researchers were racing to create the most successful biological weapons in labs like this one.

By the late 1960s, both the United States and the Soviet Union had conducted "successful" bioweapons tests. The first American field test occurred in 1969 in the Pacific Ocean and involved a fleet of ships, caged animals, and a variety of lethal agents. The U.S. Army had successfully **weaponized** a few biological agents, pairing germs with munitions and delivery systems. This involved two lethal diseases, anthrax and tularemia, and three **incapacitating** diseases, brucellosis, Q fever, and Venezuelan equine encephalitis. The United States also succeeded at creating a military-grade version of botulinum, a toxin that causes **botulism**.

Viewed under a microscope here, the bacteria that causes botulism has likely been weaponized by many countries at some point, including the United States.

Soon after, President Richard M. Nixon ended the U.S. offensive biological weapons program and ordered the destruction of all stockpiled biological agents. U.S. research efforts then focused on defense, including the development of devices to detect and defend against lethal microorganisms. In 1972, the United States and around 100 other nations signed a treaty formally called the Convention on the Prohibition of the Development, Production, and Stockpiling of Bacteriological (Biological) and Toxin Weapons and on Their Destruction. More commonly known as the Biological

UNWILLING PARTICIPANTS

Today, there are federal regulations and a serious ethical framework that guides scientific research that involves human subjects. Prior to the 1970s though, no such rules existed. Research could be done for the sake of science without regard to the effect on the subjects involved. In the case of bioweapons, this happened more than once.

In the 1950s and 1960s, U.S. officials feared being vulnerable to biological attacks. A Special Operations Division of the military was created to carry out secret field tests to determine how vulnerable the country was to germ warfare. Testing included the release of supposedly harmless bacteria from naval ships. In 1950, an experiment showed almost all of the residents of San Francisco, California, had been exposed.

In the 1960s, the tests were expanded to places such as airports and subways, all without prior consent or knowledge from the human subjects involved.

While releasing harmless bacteria without consent may not seem like much to dwell on, human-subject ethics exist for a reason. Edward Nevin was a man who passed away from an infection six months after the San Francisco test. When they learned of the testing in 1977, his family believed the "harmless" bacteria he was exposed to during the test caused his death. Ultimately, they could not prove it, but the tests remain controversial.

Weapons Convention (BWC), it was aimed at stopping countries from possessing or developing biological agents, toxins, and related weapons systems.

Despite the existence of the BWC, the Soviet Union continued to expand its biological weapons research and production programs

Cholera is a disease caused by bacteria (*shown here*) spreading in water and food supplies. In some parts of the world, it is still a problem, but other parts do not see cases of the disease anymore. The parts of the world without cholera cases do not have immunity to it and would be susceptible to an attack.

CHAPTER 2

HOW DOES GERM WARFARE WORK?

Germ warfare was originally only a serious threat from powerful governments and militaries. However, **bioterrorism** has become the new name for germ warfare that may be potentially used by terrorist groups.

In theory, any pathogenic (disease-causing) organism can be used in germ warfare. The most common weaponized pathogens are bacteria, viruses, and biological toxins. The remaining types of microbes—fungi and protozoa—are less likely to be cultivated for use in germ warfare, although some weaponized forms do exist. Even microscopic doses of some microorganisms can kill. Today, modern bioweapons require a high-level understanding of germ theory, microbiology, and the pathogens that can be used to cause disease.

BACTERIA

Bacteria are comprised of a single cell and are the smallest living organisms that can reproduce independently of a host organism. Bacteria predate human beings and other living things by a very long time: Bacterial fossils in rocks date back approximately 3.5 billion years. These early organisms are known as cyanobacteria, or blue-green algae.

Bacteria are ideal agents to be weaponized because of their remarkable adaptability to extreme environments. Bacterial diseases suitable for germ warfare include anthrax, brucellosis, cholera, tularemia, typhoid fever, and plague. All of these diseases have been developed specifically as anti-personnel weapons—made to be effective against humans.

Viruses

Viruses are the simplest microorganisms used as biological weapons. Unlike bacteria, viruses are unable to reproduce by themselves. They are little more than bits of protein that only reproduce within host cells. They aggressively colonize these other cells, alter their genetic material, and reprogram them to produce more viruses. Some viruses are spread by coughing or sneezing. Others are transmitted through blood or other bodily fluids. Smallpox and Ebola fever are examples of virus-caused diseases.

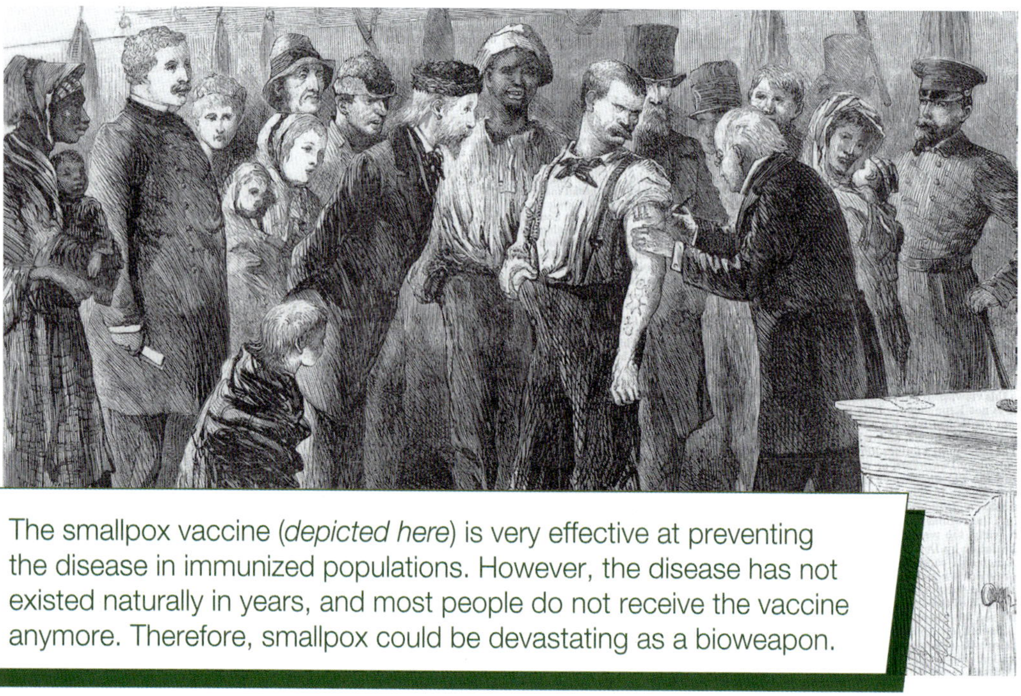

The smallpox vaccine (*depicted here*) is very effective at preventing the disease in immunized populations. However, the disease has not existed naturally in years, and most people do not receive the vaccine anymore. Therefore, smallpox could be devastating as a bioweapon.

Viruses can infect people, animals, and plants. Some infections are treatable; others are not. Antibiotics are generally ineffective against viruses, but vaccination offers some protection. A vaccine is often created using dead or weakened germs that can be killed by the body's immune system. The body then retains for some time chemicals that can recognize and destroy that particular virus.

HIGH-THREAT AGENTS

DISEASE	TIME BEFORE SYMPTOMS	SYMPTOMS
anthrax	typically 1 to 6 days, up to 42	cough, fever, sweating, fatigue, muscle pain
plague	1 to 7 days (usually 2 to 3 days)	cough, shortness of breath, sore lymph nodes, fever
tularemia	1 to 21 days (average: 3 to 6 days)	fever, cough, headache, development of pneumonia,
Marburg (viral hemorrhagic fever)	4 to 21 days	sudden onset fever, rash, headache followed by vomiting and diarrhea, generalized bleeding in severe cases
Ebola (viral hemorrhagic fever)	4 to 21 days	sudden onset fever, rash, headache followed by vomiting and diarrhea, generalized bleeding in severe cases
smallpox	7 to 17 days (average: 12 days)	fever, aches, rash appears after 2 to 4 days
botulism	12 hours to 5 days	muscle paralysis

These germs are considered high-priority, high-threat agents by the U.S. government.

Biotoxins

Biotoxins are poisonous substances produces by living organisms. While virus- and bacteria-based biological weapons produce deadly effects, they may act slowly. Biological toxins act more rapidly. The most feared biological toxin is botulinum, which produces botulism, a form of food poisoning. Botulism causes a disruption in nerve-signal transmissions, leading to paralysis and respiratory failure. It is fatal in about 65 percent of cases. Other toxins suitable for use as agents in germ warfare include ricin, derived from castor beans, and saxitoxin, produced from blue-green algae.

Bioweapon Criteria

Of course, not all bacteria, viruses, or toxins are suitable for germ warfare. To be suitable, the agent must meet certain criteria. These include:

- capability of mass production and stable storage
- ability to consistently produce a specific effect within a predictable incubation period
- ability, when dispersed, to live long enough to reach its target

For maximum effectiveness, the target population must also exhibit certain characteristics. The population should have:

- little or no immunity to the disease
- limited or no access to treatment

Methods of Delivery

Biological agents must be weaponized to be effective. This entails preparing germs for efficient and widespread dispersal. Most biological agents are disseminated in an aerosol form. These agents can also be delivered through ingestion of contaminated food or water or by insect or rodent carriers.

Biological agents inhaled into the lungs can begin to multiply, causing debilitating or fatal diseases. They are usually invisible, odorless, and tasteless, making them especially dangerous.

Once in aerosol form, the agents can be delivered in a number of ways. The 2001 anthrax attacks were done by contaminating letters with a fine, powdered form of the anthrax bacteria. The bacteria became aerosolized when the envelope or package was jostled, dispersing them into the air. Some of the more common techniques for aerosol dispersion are:

- via bomb or missile
- through the use of airplanes (like crop dusters) that fly low over cities dispersing a fine mist
- through building ventilation systems

You may have seen an airplane spreading pesticides over farmland in a method called crop dusting. This same type of process could disperse bioweapons in the case of germ warfare.

Although not as efficient as aerosol dispersion, contaminating food and water supplies is another possible delivery method. A salmonella outbreak in Oregon in 1984 was the result of the deliberate contamination of food by a Rajneeshee religious cult. Fortunately, a large-scale bioterrorist attack involving contamination of food or water is not likely because:

- The most common biological agents cannot be transmitted through food and water.
- Most of the illnesses transmitted by these methods have short-term effects (like vomiting and diarrhea) and a high rate of recovery.
- Heat and cooking destroy most biological agents.
- Current water treatment procedures both dilute and kill most bacteria.

Though it may seem too simple, boiling water can protect us from contamination. Most germs cannot survive the heat in the process.

Insects also carry deadly infections. Fleas are known carriers of both bubonic plague and spotted typhus. Mosquitoes spread malaria. The primary limitation with this method of dispersion is that

In theory, insects could spread deadly infections in a bioterrorism attack, but it is not a likely means of dispersal in modern times. It is nearly impossible to have a specific target using insects, as you cannot control where they go.

it is almost impossible to guide insects to their targets. Despite this shortcoming, animal transmission could have potentially far-reaching effects. In the mid-1300s, bubonic plague almost wiped out the European population. Flea-infested rats carrying the disease were transported to Europe from China aboard trading vessels. The fleas were then transferred to human hosts. The plague spread rapidly. In the end, between 30 and 50 percent of the population succumbed from what was later called the Black Death.

PLAGUE WARFARE

Attempts to spread bubonic plague to defeat enemies are some of the earliest examples of germ warfare. In that case, an understanding of germ theory wasn't required. In fact, germ theory didn't even exist yet. Military strategists knew one thing: Plague spread easily, and it was deadly. Through observation, they inferred that a body infected with bubonic plague could still spread disease after death, and, in this example in germ warfare, they did just that. Hurling plague-infected bodies into cities that weren't yet ravaged by plague was likely effective.

This strategy didn't require the brightest minds of the era. It did have its limitations, though. An infected body could only spread the disease to what it touched. As a method of dispersal, it wasn't very reliable. It also wasn't able to target a specific group. Men, women, and children in the area would all get sick, whether or not that was the intention. Today, germ warfare is more specific with a much deeper understanding of the agents used to create it. The criteria established is a big part of what makes today's biological weapons have such destructive capabilities.

While germ warfare has historically been a weapon of opportunity, as germs and disease exist naturally, it has evolved into a highly scientific process. The biological weapons created today are created with the purpose and capability to be weapons of mass destruction.

WHAT DO YOU THINK?

1. Why do bioweapons need to have stable storage?
2. For an effective bioweapon, why is it important for the targets to have little to no immunity to the agent?
3. Why do you think aerosolizing the most efficient way to spread a bioweapon?

Shown here is the symbol for a biological hazard, which is another name for a biological agent that is harmful to humans. Governments have developed defenses against these.

DO WE HAVE A DEFENSE?

The good news is that as the understanding of germs has increased the capability of making sophisticated bioweapons, it has also increased our ability to create treatments for the diseases caused by the germs around us. On top of that, our knowledge of how a biological attack would likely take place lets us prepare countermeasures so we would not be caught completely surprised or defenseless.

Political Defense

The international community has taken steps to slow the increase of biological weapons. Dating all the way back to 1675, with the Strasbourg Agreement, French and German armies promised not to use poison arrows in battle. The Geneva Protocol, signed in 1925, banned the use of both chemical and biological weapons. In 1972, the BWC expanded the protocol to include bans against the development, stockpiling, sale, or use of biological weapons. The 1972 BWC attempted to ban the entire class of biological weapons, and the 1993 Chemical Weapons Conventions (CWC) took a similar approach to chemical weapons.

The U.S. government has also instituted its own programs to protect against such threats. Chief among these is the National

Pharmaceutical Stockpile Program operated by the Centers for Disease Control and Protection (CDC) in Atlanta, Georgia.

The Centers for Disease Control and Prevention (CDC) is responsible for tracking, treating, and preventing public health threats in the United States, including biological warfare.

This program permits the stockpiling of medical and surgical items that would be necessary in the event of a biological or chemical attack. These items include antibiotics, antitoxins, vaccines, life-support medications, and chemical antidotes. Another initiative, largely a response to the 2001 anthrax attacks, is the installation of **irradiation** equipment at some U.S. Postal Service locations that "zap" the mail with a high-speed electron beam that can kill most microorganisms.

READY TO RESPOND

The military branches have expanded on international treaties by including in their own charters a responsibility for removing or reducing the threat of germ warfare, minimizing vulnerability to the effects of the agents, and providing defensive and protective measures, including the development of warning and reporting programs as well as detection, identification, and decontamination.

Should a biological attack occur, it is important to identify the agent and begin appropriate treatments as soon as possible. Since the majority of biological agents are colorless, odorless, and tasteless, detection devices—paper or liquids that change color in the presence of specific chemical or biological agents—are available for military use in combat areas. A Biological Integrated Detection System (BIDS) is also used by the military to detect microorganisms like those that cause anthrax and plague. Detection devices for personal use by the general public are not currently available or have suspect reliability.

Once biological agents are detected in the atmosphere, a sealed, ventilated shelter can provide some protection by preventing or delaying the agents from entering the lungs or coming into contact with the skin. If contact does occur, quick decontamination is possible for most known biological agents. Bleach and even soap and water are capable of neutralizing most agents if applied in a timely manner.

In labs, scientists wear special protective equipment when studying biohazards.

CHAPTER 4

IS GERM WARFARE STILL A THREAT?

In the modern era, the likelihood of germ warfare being carried out has been extremely low, but it still exists. Because germ warfare is so serious, even threats that turn out to be **hoaxes** are increasingly worrisome. Experts believe that more countries and terrorist groups will gain access to the technology needed to produce bioweapons. We take solace in the fact that many countries have had the means to create these weapons for decades and have not chosen to use them. The devastating capabilities of these germs must be clear. As more groups gain capabilities to create them, the threat for an attack increases. Hopefully, the horrifying effects that an agent would likely cause and risk to oneself remain strong deterrents.

THREAT OF STOCKPILES TODAY

Iraq launched a bioweapons program in 1985. Initial developments were weak and ineffective, but Iraq's scientific teams were committed. By the time of the Persian Gulf cease-fire in 1991, Iraq had weaponized large quantities of anthrax bacteria and botulinum toxin. The starter germs for these deadly agents were purchased from an American company, the American Type Culture Collection. This scientific supply company housed the world's largest collection of germ strains, including some particularly virulent strains of anthrax bacterium and botulinum, which were discovered as part of the American germ warfare development program in the mid-1950s. The collection served as a global lending library for scientists beginning research in the field of biotechnology. It was considered an essential entity in the fight to improve global health. However, using these resources, a country that was once a probable Arab ally for the United States, particularly against Iran, was being monitored for producing and possibly using biological agents.

Some experts believe that nations such as Iraq continued to engage in the production of biological weapons not for offensive use, but as defense, to compensate for their weaker military forces. To some countries, the use of biological weapons may be the only way they see to protect themselves against more powerful foes.

United Nations Investigation

In the months leading up to the Persian Gulf War, U.S. intelligence reports about Iraq's biological weapons supplies painted an alarming picture. Yet the reports would tell only part of the story. On April 3, 1991, the United Nations Security Council enacted Resolution 687 establishing the United Nations Special Commission, then known as UNSCOM. The sole purpose of this team of diplomats and specialists was to carry out immediate on-site inspections of Iraq's biological, chemical, and missile capabilities. Iraq approved the resolution, stating officially that it maintained no biological weapons programs. By August 1991, however, the first UNSCOM report would indicate the contrary.

Over the next few years, UNSCOM inspectors would uncover numerous bioweapons facilities and inaccuracies in Iraqi reports. Finally, in 1995, Iraq admitted to the production of thousands of gallons of anthrax bacterium and botulinum, initially stating that all supplies were destroyed. This statement was later recanted, and weapons inspectors were shown detailed research identifying thousands of tons of weaponized biological agents as well as the missiles to deliver them. Iraq also possessed fertilizer sprayers set aside as means for dispersing these agents.

In late 1997, Iraqi president Saddam Hussein had enough of UNSCOM's scrutiny and banned any further weapons inspections. Although Iraq claimed to have destroyed most biological agents and the weapons for delivering them, no proof was offered.

On December 17, 1999, UNSCOM was replaced with the United Nations Monitoring, Verification, and Inspection Commission (UNMOVIC). The stated mission was to continue the mandate of Resolution 687 and disarm Iraq of its weapons of mass destruction, and to maintain a system of ongoing monitoring and verification to check Iraq's compliance with its obligations. Dr. Hans Blix of Sweden was appointed the commission's executive chairman.

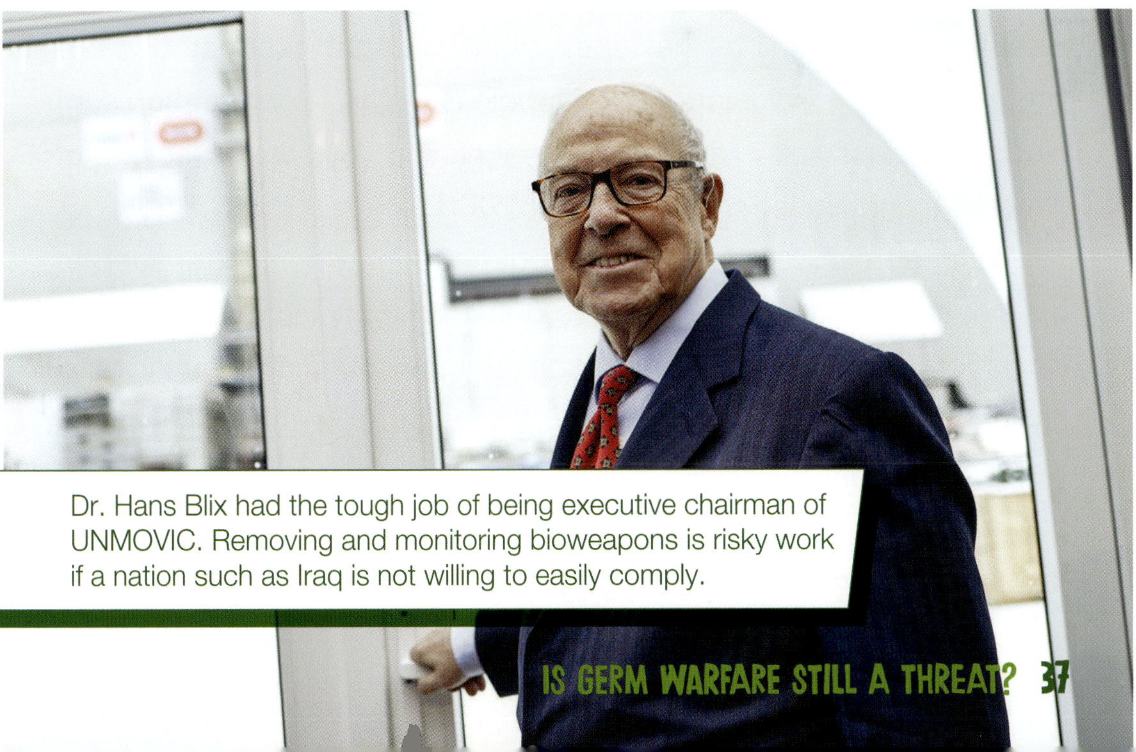

Dr. Hans Blix had the tough job of being executive chairman of UNMOVIC. Removing and monitoring bioweapons is risky work if a nation such as Iraq is not willing to easily comply.

GOING TO WAR

Shortly after the September 11, 2001, terrorist attacks on the United States, Iraq's biological weapons programs came into question again. In late 2002, President George W. Bush addressed the United Nations Security Council on this issue, and on November 8, 2002, Resolution 1441, outlining a final opportunity for Iraq to comply with its disarmament obligations, was adopted. UNMOVIC inspectors were permitted to return to Iraq on November 27, 2002, in conjunction with a team from the International Atomic Energy Agency (IAEA). Although allowed to return, the weapons inspectors were still met with resistance.

In early 2003, the United States claimed that Iraqi officials were sabotaging the search for biological and other weapons. Intelligence reports claiming that these were more than likely to exist were quoted by then-U.S. Secretary of State General Colin Powell as justification for a U.S.-led invasion to disarm Iraq. These were later discovered to be highly inaccurate, with some people even claiming that they were outright fabricated as a pretense for invasion. Nevertheless, the destruction of Saddam Hussein's regime was achieved by an invasion of American and British troops in April 2003.

No weapons were found, and a decade-long conflict ensued in Iraq, even after the United States declared early victory. For some observers, it was a demonstration of how much the public and its leaders feared biological agents and other weapons of mass destruction, that they were willing to wage preemptive war against these potential threats.

With the risk of bioweapons seemingly high, President Bush declared war on Iraq in an attempt to disarm "weapons of mass destruction."

GERM WARFARE IN POPULAR CULTURE

Ever since fictional books, television shows, games, and movies have existed, real fears have been exploited for entertainment. Germ warfare is no exception. Because we have seen so little of it in modern times, popular culture dramatizes what could be. Popular video games such as *Fallout*, *Resident Evil*, *Call of Duty*, and *Mass Effect*, among others, all have bioweapon plots. Countless movies and television series also imagine the devastation of bioterrorism, often in extremely fictional ways, such as from extraterrestrials in the *Alien* franchise, and sometimes more realistically, such as a *Criminal Minds* episode with an anthrax attack.

While exploring the threat of biological warfare through video games is likely harmless, it also emphasizes the universal fear the potential of these weapons causes. If it wasn't a true threat, it would not be a captivating, adrenaline-producing, pop culture **trope**. It is important for people to understand the threat is not entirely fictional, though; they should not live in fear, but they should understand how to be prepared.

MOVING FORWARD

Germ warfare is still a threat today and will likely continue to be a threat in the future. Any weapons that can cause mass devastation, especially those we have little control over, inspire fear. As we make new discoveries, they will almost always be used for both good and bad. New scientific discoveries are important though, even when they come with risks.

Modern biological warfare depends on the fear it inspires. The threat and existence of these germs is enough to make nations with weaker militaries feel strong and governments think twice before any potential attack.

Although the capabilities for massive attacks that would cause significant casualties are known to exist, they have not happened. Even more promising, in instances of small-scale attacks, defense and treatment strategies have been largely successful. Continuing to increase our defenses through science and medicine will likely continue to be our best strategy in the fight against bioterrorism and germ warfare.

WHAT DO YOU THINK?

1. Do you think the fear and suspicion of weapons of mass destruction, such as bioweapons, in Iraq was enough to justify invading in 2003?
2. Why do you think many threats of bioterrorism attacks turn out to be hoaxes?
3. How could creating bioweapons be a defensive strategy for some countries?

GLOSSARY

aerosol: An airborne suspension of tiny droplets or particles.

agent: Something that produces or is capable of producing an effect.

bioterrorism: The deliberate use of harmful and deadly biological agents to create and exploit fear among a target population.

biotoxin: A poison produced by a living organism, especially bacteria, capable of causing disease.

botulism: A rare but serious illness caused by a toxin that attacks the body's nerves and causes difficulty breathing, muscle paralysis, and even death.

disseminate: To spread widely.

hoax: A deception.

incapacitate: To prevent from functioning in a normal way.

irradiation: The application of ionizing radiation.

nonperishable: Packaged or processed to withstand long storage time without spoiling.

pathogen: A microorganism capable of causing disease.

stockpile: To accumulate in large quantities to store for an extended period.

trope: In the arts, a theme that is used often enough to be common and even overused.

weaponize: To match a harmful biological agent to a method of delivering it.

weapon of mass destruction: A military weapon capable of killing large numbers of people and destroying infrastructure on a mass scale.

FIND OUT MORE

BOOKS

Buteyn, Leslie. *Bioweapons*. Costa Mesa, CA: Saddleback Educational Publishing, 2018.

Rice, Earle. *Biosecurity: Preventing Biological Warfare*. New York, NY: Enslow Publishing, 2017.

WEBSITES

CDC: Bioterrorism
emergency.cdc.gov/bioterrorism
This section of the CDC website has information on specific bioterrorism agents as well as tips for preparing for a possible attack.

NOVA Online: Bioterror
pbs.org/wgbh/nova/bioterror
This is a companion website for a PBS film and includes linked information on germ warfare.

Ready
www.ready.gov
Ready is a national campaign to educate and empower Americans to prepare for, respond to, and handle natural and human-made emergencies.

ORGANIZATIONS

Association of Medical Microbiology and Infectious Disease Canada (AMMI)
192 Bank Street
Ottawa ON K2P 1W8
Canada
Email: info@ammi.ca
www.ammi.ca
AMMI promotes the prevention, diagnosis, and treatment of human infectious diseases through its involvement in education, research, clinical practice, and patient advocacy.

Centers for Disease Control and Prevention (CDC)
1600 Clifton Road
Atlanta, GA 30329
www.cdc.gov
The CDC is the primary U.S. government agency in charge of tracking, treating, and preventing public health threats, including the spread of infectious diseases.

United States Department of Homeland Security (DHS)
300 7th Street SW
Washington, D.C. 20024
www.dhs.gov
The U.S. Department of Homeland Security is the department of the federal government charged with protecting the United States and its territories from and responding to terrorist attacks, human-made accidents, and natural disasters.

Publisher's note to educators and parents: Our editors have carefully reviewed these websites to ensure that they are suitable for students. Many websites change frequently, however, and we cannot guarantee that a site's future contents will continue to meet our high standards of quality and educational value. Be advised that students should be closely supervised whenever they access the internet.

INDEX

About the Author

Kathryn Kroe has a master's degree in public health from the University at Buffalo and a bachelor's degree in education from SUNY Buffalo State College. She is passionate about spreading accurate information and helping young people understand issues pertaining to their health and the health of those around them. She currently lives in Lockport, New York, with her husband and two toddlers. She enjoys walking with her family, playing with her Australian shepherd, Zoey, and traveling to see new places.